Homer And Classical Philology

Friedrich Nietzsche

[ZHINGOORA BOOKS]

This edition is published by
Zhingoora Books.

Apart from any fair dealing for the purposes of research or private study, or criti-cism or review, this publication may only be reproduced, stored or transmitted, in any form or by any means, with the prior permission in writing of the publishers. All disputes are subject to exclusive jurisdiction of Mandsaur Courts only. For any suggestions and feedback or book on new concept/domain, please contact us at the email given below.

contact@Zhingoora.com

HOMER AND CLASSICAL PHILOLOGY.

(Inaugural Address delivered at Bâle University, 28th of May 1869.)

At the present day no clear and consistent opinion seems to be held regarding Classical Philology. We are conscious of this in the circles of the learned just as much as among the followers of that science itself. The cause of this lies in its many-sided character, in the lack of an abstract unity, and in the inorganic aggregation of heterogeneous scientific activities which are connected with one another only by the name "Philology." It must be freely admitted that philology is to some extent borrowed from several other sciences, and is mixed together like a magic potion from the most outlandish liquors, ores, and bones. It may even be added that it likewise conceals within itself an artistic element, one which, on æsthetic and ethical grounds, may be called imperatival—an element that acts in opposition to its purely scientific behaviour. Philology is composed of history just as much as of natural science or æsthetics: history, in so far as it endeavours to comprehend the manifestations of the individualities of peoples in ever new images, and the prevailing law in the disappearance of phenomena; natural science, in so far as it strives to fathom the deepest instinct of man, that of speech; æsthetics, finally, because from various antiquities at our disposal it endeavours to pick out the so-called "classical" antiquity, with the view and pretension of excavating the ideal world buried under it, and to hold up to the present the mirror of the classical and everlasting standards. That these wholly different scientific and æsthetico-ethical impulses have been associated under a common name, a kind of sham monarchy, is shown especially by the fact that philology at every period from its origin onwards was at the same time pedagogical. From the standpoint of the pedagogue, a choice was offered of those elements which were of the greatest educational value; and thus that science, or at least that scientific aim, which we call philology, gradually developed out of the practical calling originated by the exigencies of that science itself.

These philological aims were pursued sometimes with greater ardour and sometimes with less, in accordance with the degree of culture and the development of the taste of a particular period; but, on the other hand, the followers of this science are in the habit of regarding the aims which correspond to their several abilities as *the* aims of philology; whence it comes about that the estimation of philology in public opinion depends upon the weight of the personalities of the philologists!

At the present time—that is to say, in a period which has seen men distinguished in almost every department of philology—a general uncertainty of judgment has increased more and more, and likewise a general relaxation of interest and participation in philological problems. Such an undecided and imperfect state of public opinion is damaging to a science in that its hidden and open enemies can work with much better prospects of success. And philology has a great many such enemies. Where do we not meet with them, these mockers, always ready to aim a blow at the philological "moles," the animals that practise dust-eating *ex professo*, and that grub up and eat for the eleventh time what they have already eaten ten times before. For opponents of this sort, however, philology is merely a useless, harmless, and inoffensive pastime, an object of laughter and not of hate. But, on the other hand, there is a boundless and infuriated hatred of philology wherever an ideal, as such, is feared, where the modern man falls down to worship himself, and where Hellenism is looked upon as a superseded and hence very insignificant point of view. Against these enemies, we philologists must always count upon the assistance of artists and men of artistic minds; for they alone can judge how the sword of barbarism sweeps over the head of every one who loses sight of the unutterable simplicity and noble dignity of the Hellene; and how no progress in commerce or technical industries, however brilliant, no school regulations, no political education of the masses, however widespread and complete, can protect us from the curse of ridiculous and barbaric offences against good taste, or from annihilation by the Gorgon head of the classicist.

Whilst philology as a whole is looked on with jealous eyes by these two classes of opponents, there are numerous and varied hostilities in other directions of philology; philologists themselves are quarrelling with one another; internal dissensions are caused by useless disputes about precedence and mutual jealousies, but especially by the differences—even enmities—comprised in the name of philology, which are not, however, by any means naturally harmonised instincts.

Science has this in common with art, that the most ordinary, everyday thing appears to it as something entirely new and attractive, as if metamorphosed by witchcraft and now seen for the first time. Life is worth living, says art, the beautiful temptress; life is worth knowing, says science. With this contrast the so heartrending and dogmatic tradition follows in a *theory*, and consequently in the practice of classical philology derived from this theory. We may consider antiquity from a scientific point of view; we may try to look at what has happened with the eye of a historian, or to arrange and compare the linguistic forms of ancient masterpieces, to bring them at all events under a morphological law; but we always lose the wonderful creative force, the real fragrance, of the atmosphere of antiquity; we forget that passionate emotion which instinctively drove our meditation and enjoyment back to the Greeks. From this point onwards we must take notice of a clearly determined and very surprising antagonism which philology has great cause to regret. From the circles upon whose help we must place the most implicit reliance—the artistic friends of antiquity, the warm supporters of Hellenic beauty and noble simplicity—we hear harsh voices crying out that it is precisely the philologists themselves who are the real opponents and destroyers of the ideals of antiquity. Schiller upbraided the philologists with having scattered Homer's laurel crown to the winds. It was none other than Goethe who, in early life a supporter of Wolf's theories regarding Homer, recanted in the verses—

With subtle wit you took away
Our former adoration:
The Iliad, you may us say,
Was mere conglomeration.
Think it not crime in any way:
Youth's fervent adoration
Leads us to know the verity,
And feel the poet's unity.

The reason of this want of piety and reverence must lie deeper; and many are in doubt as to whether philologists are lacking in artistic capacity and impressions, so that they are unable to do justice to the ideal, or whether the spirit of negation has become a destructive and iconoclastic principle of theirs. When, however, even the friends of antiquity, possessed of such doubts and hesitations, point to our present classical philology as something questionable, what influence may we not ascribe to the outbursts of the "realists" and the claptrap of the heroes of the passing hour? To answer the latter on this occasion, especially when we consider the nature of the present assembly, would be highly injudicious; at any rate, if I do not wish to meet with the fate of that sophist who, when in Sparta, publicly undertook to praise and defend Herakles, when he was interrupted with the query: "But who then has found fault with him?" I cannot help thinking, however, that some of these scruples are still sounding in the ears of not a few in this gathering; for they may still be frequently heard from the lips of noble and artistically gifted men— as even an upright philologist must feel them, and feel them most painfully, at moments when his spirits are downcast. For the single individual there is no deliverance from the dissensions referred to; but what we contend and inscribe on our banner is the fact that classical philology, as a whole, has nothing whatsoever to do with the quarrels and bickerings of its individual disciples. The entire scientific and artistic movement of this peculiar centaur is bent, though with cyclopic slowness, upon bridging over the gulf between the ideal antiquity—which is perhaps only the magnificent blossoming of the Teutonic longing for the south—and the real antiquity; and thus classical philology pursues only the final end of its own being, which is the fusing together of primarily hostile impulses that have only forcibly been brought together. Let us talk as we will about the unattainability of this goal, and even designate the goal itself as an illogical pretension—the aspiration for it is very real; and I should like to try to make it clear by an example that the most significant steps of classical philology never lead away from the ideal antiquity, but to it; and that, just when people are speaking unwarrantably of the overthrow of sacred shrines, new and more worthy altars are being erected. Let us then examine the so-called *Homeric question* from this standpoint, a question the most important problem of which Schiller called a scholastic barbarism.

The important problem referred to is *the question of the personality of Homer.*

We now meet everywhere with the firm opinion that the question of Homer's personality is no longer timely, and that it is quite a different thing from the real "Homeric question." It may be added that, for a given period—such as our present philological period, for example—the centre of discussion may be removed from the problem of the poet's personality; for even now a painstaking experiment is being made to reconstruct the Homeric poems without the aid of personality, treating them as the work of several different persons. But if the centre of a scientific question is rightly seen to be where the swelling tide of new views has risen up, *i.e.* where individual scientific investigation comes into contact with the whole life of science and culture—if any one, in other words, indicates a historico-cultural valuation as the central point of the question, he must also, in the province of Homeric criticism, take his stand upon the question of personality as being the really fruitful oasis in the desert of the whole argument. For in Homer the modern world, I will not say has learnt, but has examined, a great historical point of view; and, even without now putting forward my own opinion as to whether this examination has been or can be happily carried out, it was at all events the first example of the application of that productive point of view. By it scholars learnt to recognise condensed beliefs in the apparently firm, immobile figures of the life of ancient peoples; by it they for the first time perceived the wonderful capability of the soul of a people to represent the conditions of its morals and beliefs in the form of a personality. When historical criticism has confidently seized upon this method of evaporating apparently concrete personalities, it is permissible to point to the first experiment as an important event in the history of sciences, without considering whether it was successful in this instance or not.

It is a common occurrence for a series of striking signs and wonderful emotions to precede an epoch-making discovery. Even the experiment I have just referred to has its own attractive history; but it goes back to a surprisingly ancient era. Friedrich August Wolf has exactly indicated the spot where Greek antiquity dropped the question. The zenith of the historico-literary studies of the Greeks, and hence also of their point of greatest importance—the Homeric question—was reached in the age of the Alexandrian grammarians. Up to this time the Homeric question had run through the long chain of a uniform process of development, of which the standpoint of those grammarians seemed to be the last link, the last, indeed, which was attainable by antiquity. They conceived the *Iliad* and the *Odyssey* as the creations of *one single* Homer; they declared it to be psychologically possible for two such different works to have sprung from the brain of *one* genius, in contradiction to the Chorizontes, who represented the extreme limit of the scepticism of a few detached individuals of antiquity rather than antiquity itself considered as a whole. To explain the different general impression of the two books on the assumption that *one* poet composed them both, scholars sought assistance by referring to the seasons of the poet's life, and compared the poet of the *Odyssey* to the setting sun. The eyes of those critics were tirelessly on the lookout for discrepancies in the language and thoughts of the two poems; but at this time also a history of the Homeric poem and its tradition was prepared, according to which these discrepancies were not due to Homer, but to those who committed his words to writing and those who sang them. It was believed that Homer's poem was passed from one generation to another *viva voce,* and faults were attributed to the improvising and at times forgetful bards. At a certain given date, about the time of Pisistratus, the poems which had been repeated orally were said to have been collected in manuscript form; but the scribes, it is added, allowed themselves to take some liberties with the text by transposing some lines and adding extraneous matter here and there. This entire hypothesis is the most important in the domain of literary studies that antiquity has exhibited; and the acknowledgment of the dissemination of the Homeric poems by word of mouth, as opposed to the habits of a book-learned age, shows in particular a depth of ancient sagacity worthy of our admiration. From those times until the generation that produced Friedrich August Wolf we must take a jump over a long historical vacuum; but in our own age we find the argument left just as it was at the time when the power of controversy departed from antiquity, and it is a matter of indifference to us that Wolf accepted as certain tradition what antiquity itself had set up only as a hypothesis. It may be remarked as most characteristic of this hypothesis that, in the strictest sense, the personality of Homer is treated seriously; that a certain standard of inner harmony is everywhere presupposed in the manifestations of the personality; and that, with these two excellent auxiliary hypotheses, whatever is seen to be below this standard and opposed to this inner harmony is at once swept aside as un-Homeric. But even this distinguishing characteristic, in place of wishing to recognise the supernatural existence of a tangible personality, ascends likewise through all the stages that lead to that zenith, with ever-increasing energy and clearness. Individuality is ever more strongly felt and accentuated; the psychological possibility of a *single* Homer is ever more forcibly demanded. If we descend backwards from this zenith, step by step, we find a guide to the understanding of the Homeric problem in the person of Aristotle. Homer was for him the flawless and untiring artist who knew his end and the means to attain it; but there is still a trace of infantile criticism to be found in Aristotle—*i.e.*, in the naive concession he made to the public opinion that considered Homer as the author of the original of all comic epics, the *Margites*. If we go still further backwards from Aristotle, the inability to create a personality is seen to increase; more and more poems are attributed to Homer; and every period lets us see its degree of criticism by how much and what it considers as Homeric. In this backward examination, we instinctively feel that away beyond Herodotus there lies a period in which an immense flood of great epics has been identified with the name of Homer.

Let us imagine ourselves as living in the time of Pisistratus: the word "Homer" then comprehended an abundance of dissimilarities. What was meant by "Homer" at that time? It is evident that that generation found itself unable to grasp a personality and the limits of its manifestations. Homer had now become of small consequence. And then we meet with the weighty question: What lies before this period? Has Homer's personality, because it cannot be grasped, gradually faded away into an empty name? Or had all the Homeric poems been gathered together in a body, the nation naively representing itself by the figure of Homer? *Was the person created out of a conception, or the conception out of a person?* This is the real "Homeric question," the central problem of the personality.

The difficulty of answering this question, however, is increased when we seek a reply in another direction, from the standpoint of the poems themselves which have come down to us. As it is difficult for us at the present day, and necessitates a serious effort on our part, to understand the law of gravitation clearly—that the earth alters its form of motion when another heavenly body changes its position in space, although no material connection unites one to the other—it likewise costs us some trouble to obtain a clear impression of that wonderful problem which, like a coin long passed from hand to hand, has lost its original and highly conspicuous stamp. Poetical works, which cause the hearts of even the greatest geniuses to fail when they endeavour to vie with them, and in which unsurpassable images are held up for the admiration of posterity—and yet the poet who wrote them with only a hollow, shaky name, whenever we do lay hold on him; nowhere the solid kernel of a powerful personality. "For who would wage war with the gods: who, even with the one god?" asks Goethe even, who, though a genius, strove in vain to solve that mysterious problem of the Homeric inaccessibility.

The conception of popular poetry seemed to lead like a bridge over this problem—a deeper and more original power than that of every single creative individual was said to have become active; the happiest people, in the happiest period of its existence, in the highest activity of fantasy and formative power, was said to have created those immeasurable poems. In this universality there is something almost intoxicating in the thought of a popular poem: we feel, with artistic pleasure, the broad, overpowering liberation of a popular gift, and we delight in this natural phenomenon as we do in an uncontrollable cataract. But as soon as we examine this thought at close quarters, we involuntarily put a poetic *mass of people* in the place of the poetising *soul of the people*: a long row of popular poets in whom individuality has no meaning, and in whom the tumultuous movement of a people's soul, the intuitive strength of a people's eye, and the unabated profusion of a people's fantasy, were once powerful: a row of original geniuses, attached to a time, to a poetic genus, to a subject-matter.

Such a conception justly made people suspicious. Could it be possible that that same Nature who so sparingly distributed her rarest and most precious production—genius—should suddenly take the notion of lavishing her gifts in one sole direction? And here the thorny question again made its appearance: Could we not get along with one genius only, and explain the present existence of that unattainable excellence? And now eyes were keenly on the lookout for whatever that excellence and singularity might consist of. Impossible for it to be in the construction of the complete works, said one party, for this is far from faultless; but doubtless to be found in single songs: in the single pieces above all; not in the whole. A second party, on the other hand, sheltered themselves beneath the authority of Aristotle, who especially admired Homer's "divine" nature in the choice of his entire subject, and the manner in which he planned and carried it out. If, however, this construction was not clearly seen, this fault was due to the way the poems were handed down to posterity and not to the poet himself—it was the result of retouchings and interpolations, owing to which the original setting of the work gradually became obscured. The more the first school looked for inequalities, contradictions, perplexities, the more energetically did the other school brush aside what in their opinion obscured the original plan, in order, if possible, that nothing might be left remaining but the actual words of the original epic itself. The second school of thought of course held fast by the conception of an epoch-making genius as the composer of the great works. The first school, on the other hand, wavered between the supposition of one genius plus a number of minor poets, and another hypothesis which assumed only a number of superior and even mediocre individual bards, but also postulated a mysterious discharging, a deep, national, artistic impulse, which shows itself in individual minstrels as an almost indifferent medium. It is to this latter school that we must attribute the representation of the Homeric poems as the expression of that mysterious impulse.

All these schools of thought start from the assumption that the problem of the present form of these epics can be solved from the standpoint of an æsthetic judgment—but we must await the decision as to the authorised line of demarcation between the man of genius and the poetical soul of the people. Are there characteristic differences between the utterances of the *man of genius* and the *poetical soul of the people*?

This whole contrast, however, is unjust and misleading. There is no more dangerous assumption in modern æsthetics than that of *popular poetry* and *individual poetry*, or, as it is usually called, *artistic poetry*. This is the reaction, or, if you will, the superstition, which followed upon the most momentous discovery of historico-philological science, the discovery and appreciation of the *soul of the people*. For this discovery prepared the way for a coming scientific view of history, which was until then, and in many respects is even now, a mere collection of materials, with the prospect that new materials would continue to be added, and that the huge, overflowing pile would never be systematically arranged. The people now understood for the first time that the long-felt power of greater individualities and wills was larger than the pitifully small will of an individual man;[1] they now saw that everything truly great in the kingdom of the will could not have its deepest root in the inefficacious and ephemeral individual will; and, finally, they now discovered the powerful instincts of the masses, and diagnosed those unconscious impulses to be the foundations and supports of the so-called universal history. But the newly-lighted flame also cast its shadow: and this shadow was none other than that superstition already referred to, which popular poetry set up in opposition to individual poetry, and thus enlarged the comprehension of the people's soul to that of the people's mind. By the misapplication of a tempting analogical inference, people had reached the point of applying in the domain of the intellect and artistic ideas that principle of greater individuality which is truly applicable only in the domain of the will. The masses have never experienced more flattering treatment than in thus having the laurel of genius set upon their empty heads. It was imagined that new shells were forming round a small kernel, so to speak, and that those pieces of popular poetry originated like avalanches, in the drift and flow of tradition. They were, however, ready to consider that kernel as being of the smallest possible dimensions, so that they might occasionally get rid of it altogether without losing anything of the mass of the avalanche. According to this view, the text itself and the stories built round it are one and the same thing.

[1]Of course Nietzsche saw afterwards that this was not so.—TR.

Now, however, such a contrast between popular poetry and individual poetry does not exist at all; on the contrary, all poetry, and of course popular poetry also, requires an intermediary individuality. This much-abused contrast, therefore, is necessary only when the term *individual poem* is understood to mean a poem which has not grown out of the soil of popular feeling, but which has been composed by a non-popular poet in a non-popular atmosphere—something which has come to maturity in the study of a learned man, for example.

With the superstition which presupposes poetising masses is connected another: that popular poetry is limited to one particular period of a people's history and afterwards dies out—which indeed follows as a consequence of the first superstition I have mentioned. According to this school, in the place of the gradually decaying popular poetry we have artistic poetry, the work of individual minds, not of masses of people. But the same powers which were once active are still so; and the form in which they act has remained exactly the same. The great poet of a literary period is still a popular poet in no narrower sense than the popular poet of an illiterate age. The difference between them is not in the way they originate, but it is their diffusion and propagation, in short, *tradition*. This tradition is exposed to eternal danger without the help of handwriting, and runs the risk of including in the poems the remains of those individualities through whose oral tradition they were handed down.

If we apply all these principles to the Homeric poems, it follows that we gain nothing with our theory of the poetising soul of the people, and that we are always referred back to the poetical individual. We are thus confronted with the task of distinguishing that which can have originated only in a single poetical mind from that which is, so to speak, swept up by the tide of oral tradition, and which is a highly important constituent part of the Homeric poems.

Since literary history first ceased to be a mere collection of names, people have attempted to grasp and formulate the individualities of the poets. A certain mechanism forms part of the method: it must be explained—*i.e.*, it must be deduced from principles—why this or that individuality appears in this way and not in that. People now study biographical details, environment, acquaintances, contemporary events, and believe that by mixing all these ingredients together they will be able to manufacture the wished-for individuality. But they forget that the *punctum saliens*, the indefinable individual characteristics, can never be obtained from a compound of this nature. The less there is known about the life and times of the poet, the less applicable is this mechanism. When, however, we have merely the works and the name of the writer, it is almost impossible to detect the individuality, at all events, for those who put their faith in the mechanism in question; and particularly when the works are perfect, when they are pieces of popular poetry. For the best way for these mechanicians to grasp individual characteristics is by perceiving deviations from the genius of the people; the aberrations and hidden allusions: and the fewer discrepancies to be found in a poem the fainter will be the traces of the individual poet who composed it.

All those deviations, everything dull and below the ordinary standard which scholars think they perceive in the Homeric poems, were attributed to tradition, which thus became the scapegoat. What was left of Homer's own individual work? Nothing but a series of beautiful and prominent passages chosen in accordance with subjective taste. The sum total of æsthetic singularity which every individual scholar perceived with his own artistic gifts, he now called Homer.

This is the central point of the Homeric errors. The name of Homer, from the very beginning, has no connection either with the conception of æsthetic perfection or yet with the *Iliad* and the *Odyssey*. Homer as the composer of the *Iliad* and the *Odyssey* is not a historical tradition, but an *æsthetic judgment*.

The only path which leads back beyond the time of Pisistratus and helps us to elucidate the meaning of the name Homer, takes its way on the one hand through the reports which have reached us concerning Homer's birthplace: from which we see that, although his name is always associated with heroic epic poems, he is on the other hand no more referred to as the composer of the *Iliad* and the *Odyssey* than as the author of the *Thebais* or any other cyclical epic. On the other hand, again, an old tradition tells of the contest between Homer and Hesiod, which proves that when these two names were mentioned people instinctively thought of two epic tendencies, the heroic and the didactic; and that the signification of the name "Homer" was included in the material category and not in the formal. This imaginary contest with Hesiod did not even yet show the faintest presentiment of individuality. From the time of Pisistratus onwards, however, with the surprisingly rapid development of the Greek feeling for beauty, the differences in the æsthetic value of those epics continued to be felt more and more: the *Iliad* and the *Odyssey* arose from the depths of the flood and have remained on the surface ever since. With this process of æsthetic separation, the conception of Homer gradually became narrower: the old material meaning of the name "Homer" as the father of the heroic epic poem, was changed into the æsthetic meaning of Homer, the father of poetry in general, and likewise its original prototype. This transformation was contemporary with the rationalistic criticism which made Homer the magician out to be a possible poet, which vindicated the material and formal traditions of those numerous epics as against the unity of the poet, and gradually removed that heavy load of cyclical epics from Homer's shoulders.

So Homer, the poet of the *Iliad* and the *Odyssey*, is an æsthetic judgment. It is, however, by no means affirmed against the poet of these epics that he was merely the imaginary being of an æsthetic impossibility, which can be the opinion of only very few philologists indeed. The majority contend that a single individual was responsible for the general design of a poem such as the *Iliad*, and further that this individual was Homer. The first part of this contention may be admitted; but, in accordance with what I have said, the latter part must be denied. And I very much doubt whether the majority of those who adopt the first part of the contention have taken the following considerations into account.

The design of an epic such as the *Iliad* is not an entire *whole*, not an organism; but a number of pieces strung together, a collection of reflections arranged in accordance with æsthetic rules. It is certainly the standard of an artist's greatness to note what he can take in with a single glance and set out in rhythmical form. The infinite profusion of images and incidents in the Homeric epic must force us to admit that such a wide range of vision is next to impossible. Where, however, a poet is unable to observe artistically with a single glance, he usually piles conception on conception, and endeavours to adjust his characters according to a comprehensive scheme.

He will succeed in this all the better the more he is familiar with the fundamental principles of æsthetics: he will even make some believe that he made himself master of the entire subject by a single powerful glance.

The *Iliad* is not a garland, but a bunch of flowers. As many pictures as possible are crowded on one canvas; but the man who placed them there was indifferent as to whether the grouping of the collected pictures was invariably suitable and rhythmically beautiful. He well knew that no one would ever consider the collection as a whole; but would merely look at the individual parts. But that stringing together of some pieces as the manifestations of a grasp of art which was not yet highly developed, still less thoroughly comprehended and generally esteemed, cannot have been the real Homeric deed, the real Homeric epoch-making event. On the contrary, this design is a later product, far later than Homer's celebrity. Those, therefore, who look for the "original and perfect design" are looking for a mere phantom; for the dangerous path of oral tradition had reached its end just as the systematic arrangement appeared on the scene; the disfigurements which were caused on the way could not have affected the design, for this did not form part of the material handed down from generation to generation.

The relative imperfection of the design must not, however, prevent us from seeing in the designer a different personality from the real poet. It is not only probable that everything which was created in those times with conscious æsthetic insight, was infinitely inferior to the songs that sprang up naturally in the poet's mind and were written down with instinctive power: we can even take a step further. If we include the so-called cyclic poems in this comparison, there remains for the designer of the *Iliad* and the *Odyssey* the indisputable merit of having done something relatively great in this conscious technical composing: a merit which we might have been prepared to recognise from the beginning, and which is in my opinion of the very first order in the domain of instinctive creation. We may even be ready to pronounce this synthetisation of great importance. All those dull passages and discrepancies—deemed of such importance, but really only subjective, which we usually look upon as the petrified remains of the period of tradition—are not these perhaps merely the almost necessary evils which must fall to the lot of the poet of genius who undertakes a composition virtually without a parallel, and, further, one which proves to be of incalculable difficulty?

Let it be noted that the insight into the most diverse operations of the instinctive and the conscious changes the position of the Homeric problem; and in my opinion throws light upon it.

We believe in a great poet as the author of the *Iliad* and the *Odyssey—but not that Homer was this poet.*

The decision on this point has already been given. The generation that invented those numerous Homeric fables, that poetised the myth of the contest between Homer and Hesiod, and looked upon all the poems of the epic cycle as Homeric, did not feel an æsthetic but a material singularity when it pronounced the name "Homer." This period regards Homer as belonging to the ranks of artists like Orpheus, Eumolpus, Dædalus, and Olympus, the mythical discoverers of a new branch of art, to whom, therefore, all the later fruits which grew from the new branch were thankfully dedicated.

And that wonderful genius to whom we owe the *Iliad* and the *Odyssey* belongs to this thankful posterity: he, too, sacrificed his name on the altar of the primeval father of the Homeric epic, Homeros.

Up to this point, gentlemen, I think I have been able to put before you the fundamental philosophical and æsthetic characteristics of the problem of the personality of Homer, keeping all minor details rigorously at a distance, on the supposition that the primary form of this widespread and honeycombed mountain known as the Homeric question can be most clearly observed by looking down at it from a far-off height. But I have also, I imagine, recalled two facts to those friends of antiquity who take such delight in accusing us philologists of lack of piety for great conceptions and an unproductive zeal for destruction. In the first place, those "great" conceptions—such, for example, as that of the indivisible and inviolable poetic genius, Homer—were during the pre-Wolfian period only too great, and hence inwardly altogether empty and elusive when we now try to grasp them. If classical philology goes back again to the same conceptions, and once more tries to pour new wine into old bottles, it is only on the surface that the conceptions are the same: everything has really become new; bottle and mind, wine and word. We everywhere find traces of the fact that philology has lived in company with poets, thinkers, and artists for the last hundred years: whence it has now come about that the heap of ashes formerly pointed to as classical philology is now turned into fruitful and even rich soil.[2]

[2] Nietzsche perceived later on that this statement was, unfortunately, not justified.—TR.

And there is a second fact which I should like to recall to the memory of those friends of antiquity who turn their dissatisfied backs on classical philology. You honour the immortal masterpieces of the Hellenic mind in poetry and sculpture, and think yourselves so much more fortunate than preceding generations, which had to do without them; but you must not forget that this whole fairyland once lay buried under mountains of prejudice, and that the blood and sweat and arduous labour of innumerable followers of our science were all necessary to lift up that world from the chasm into which it had sunk. We grant that philology is not the creator of this world, not the composer of that immortal music; but is it not a merit, and a great merit, to be a mere virtuoso, and let the world for the first time hear that music which lay so long in obscurity, despised and undecipherable? Who was Homer previously to Wolf's brilliant investigations? A good old man, known at best as a "natural genius," at all events the child of a barbaric age, replete with faults against good taste and good morals. Let us hear how a learned man of the first rank writes about Homer even so late as 1783: "Where does the good man live? Why did he remain so long incognito? Apropos, can't you get me a silhouette of him?"

We demand *thanks*—not in our own name, for we are but atoms—but in the name of philology itself, which is indeed neither a Muse nor a Grace, but a messenger of the gods: and just as the Muses descended upon the dull and tormented Bœotian peasants, so Philology comes into a world full of gloomy colours and pictures, full of the deepest, most incurable woes; and speaks to men comfortingly of the beautiful and godlike figure of a distant, rosy, and happy fairyland.

It is time to close; yet before I do so a few words of a personal character must be added, justified, I hope, by the occasion of this lecture.

It is but right that a philologist should describe his end and the means to it in the short formula of a confession of faith; and let this be done in the saying of Seneca which I thus reverse—

"Philosophia facta est quæ philologia fuit."

By this I wish to signify that all philological activities should be enclosed and surrounded by a philosophical view of things, in which everything individual and isolated is evaporated as something detestable, and in which great homogeneous views alone remain. Now, therefore, that I have enunciated my philological creed, I trust you will give me cause to hope that I shall no longer be a stranger among you: give me the assurance that in working with you towards this end I am worthily fulfilling the confidence with which the highest authorities of this community have honoured me.

The End